WHO PROTESTED AGAINST THE VIETNAM WAR?

Richard Spilsbury

raintree
a Capstone company — publishers for children

Raintree is an imprint of Capstone Global
Library Limited, a company incorporated
in England and Wales having its registered
office at 7 Pilgrim Street, London, EC4V 6LB
– Registered company number: 6695582

www.raintreepublishers.co.uk
myorders@raintreepublishers.co.uk

Edited by Andrew Farrow, Patrick Catel, and
  Vaarunika Dharmapala
Designed by Steve Mead
Original illustrations © Capstone Global
  Library Ltd 2014
Illustrated by HL Studios
Picture research by Ruth Blair
Originated by Capstone Global Library Ltd
Printed in China

ISBN 978 1 406 27313 7 (hardback)
17 16 15 14 13
10 9 8 7 6 5 4 3 2 1

ISBN 978 1 406 27320 5 (paperback)
18 17 16 15 14
10 9 8 7 6 5 4 3 2 1

British Library Cataloguing in Publication Data

Spilsbury, Richard
Who protested against the Vietnam War?
(Primary source detectives)
A full catalogue record for this book is
available from the British Library.

Acknowledgements
We would like to thank the following for
permission to reproduce photographs:
Alamy pp. 16 (© Everett Collection Inc), 49
(© ZUMA Press, Inc.), 54 (© BigPileStock);
Corbis pp. 4, 6, 10, 14, 26 & 34 (© Bettmann),
31 (© Wally McNamee), 42 (© Henry Diltz),
56 (© Krista Kennell/ZUMA Press); © Corbis
p. 9; Getty Images pp. 12 (Dick Swanson//
Time Life Pictures), 20 (Denver Post), 32
(Hulton Archive), 41 (CBS Photo Archive), 44
(Redferns), 46 (Fairfax Media), 51 (Richard
Ellis), 52 (AFP); PA Photos p. 36 (Nick Ut/
AP); Reuters p. 25 (Jim Watson); Topfoto
pp. 22 & 28 (ImageWorks), 38 (The Granger
Collection); © Topfoto p. 18.

Cover photograph of Vietnam War protest
reproduced with permission of Corbis (©
Wally McNamee).

Every effort has been made to contact
copyright holders of material reproduced in
this book. Any omissions will be rectified in
subsequent printings if notice is given to the
publisher.

CONTENTS

Some words are shown in bold, **like this**. You can find out what they mean by looking in the glossary.

MARCHING ON THE WHITE HOUSE

It is 15 November 1969 in Washington, DC. A crowd of over 250,000 people have converged on the city, making this the biggest single anti-war demonstration in US history. The Vietnam **Moratorium** movement had organized the march. *Moratorium* means a suspension of activity, and the group aimed to force the US government to stop its military activity in Vietnam. The Vietnam War had been raging since around 1965, and its costs to the Vietnamese people, to US soldiers, and the US economy were becoming widely known in the United States by the late 1960s.

▼ These marchers in 1969 represented a wide cross-section of Americans strongly opposed to their country's war in Vietnam.

GROWING PROTESTS

Protests against the war had been growing in frequency and popularity. The Washington March organizers had promoted the event nationwide to encourage more protesters. David Wilcomb recalls, "Nine friends and I pooled our money, crowded into a Ford van, and drove all the way from Oklahoma to DC..."

Organizers provided free meals and lodgings at Washington schools, churches, and other organizations. Police and troops stationed around Washington watched the crowds carefully and were ready to defend the capital if they considered that the protests were out of hand.

DAY AND NIGHT PROTESTS

By day, politicians, soldiers with first-hand experience of war, students, families, and other people from all walks of life grouped by the White House to hear speeches against the Vietnam War. They sang along together to popular anti-war songs such as John Lennon's "Give Peace a Chance". **Hippies** with long hair and colourful clothes pushed flowers into soldiers' guns as a symbol of peace, while crowds including business people such as shopkeepers looked on approvingly. By night, protesters gathered in front of the White House gates. They laid out empty coffins representing some of the 45,000 US soldiers who had been killed in the Vietnam War so far. Protesters took part in a candlelit vigil in which they read out the names of some of the dead soldiers.

SUCCESS?

President Nixon claimed that a small but vocal minority of protesters was drowning out a silent majority who approved of the war. But to many people who had been at the march, read newspaper reports, or seen TV coverage, the Washington March demonstrated widespread support for the anti-war movement. As we shall see, this march and many other protests had a major impact on US involvement in Vietnam.

> At the time my judgment was that the moratorium hadn't really succeeded because the war didn't end, but ... it ... brought in people who hadn't been involved in [anti-war activity] before... In that sense it was a tremendous success.

Sam Brown, Vietnam Moratorium movement activist, 1982

HOW DID THE VIETNAM WAR BEGIN?

Imagine you were a student at college or an adult at work getting the news that you had to leave your normal life and go to the jungles of Vietnam to fight for your country. This was the reality for thousands of ordinary Americans in the mid-1960s until the early 1970s. But how did the United States and other countries become involved in the war?

▲ US soldiers crowd on to the decks of a troop ship arriving in Vietnam.

PRELUDE TO WAR

Since the late 1940s, the United States had been involved in the **Cold War** with the **USSR** and China. The United States was trying to prevent the spread of **communism**. Vietnam had been split in two in the mid-1950s, following the end of long-term **colonization** by France. A civil war had then started. North Vietnam had a popular communist leader, Ho Chi Minh, who received support and military aid from the USSR and China. South Vietnam had corrupt, unpopular, but anti-communist leadership. The United States sent military advisors to help South Vietnamese forces so they might beat the enemy – the North Vietnamese Army (PAVN) and the South Vietnamese National Liberation Front rebels, often called the **Vietcong**. The United States was concerned that if Vietnam became communist, surrounding countries such as Cambodia and Laos might become communist too, and communism would spread through Asia. This was known as the domino effect.

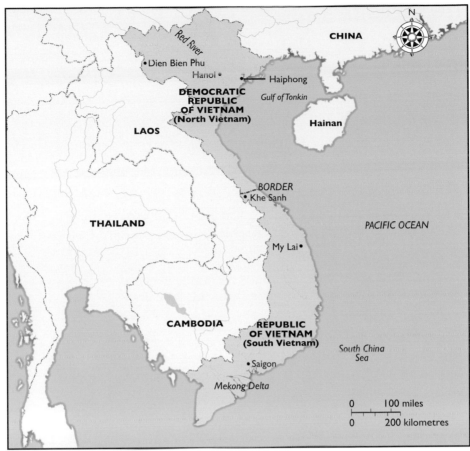

▲ By the mid-1960s, Vietnam was divided into two opposing halves and locked in a bitter civil war.

TO WAR

By the mid-1960s, Americans felt they needed to become directly involved to beat Ho Chi Minh's forces. In 1964, US Navy ships patrolling in an area of the South China Sea called the Gulf of Tonkin claimed that North Vietnamese forces had attacked them. In response, Congress passed the Gulf of Tonkin resolution, authorizing President Johnson "to take all necessary measures to repel any armed attack against the forces of United States and to prevent further aggression".

US aeroplanes and naval ships started a massive bombing campaign in North and South Vietnam, but the destruction encouraged many Vietnamese to join the Vietcong. In 1965, the United States decided to send in 100,000 troops to help the South Vietnamese win.

NEW RECRUITS

A member of the US army is a GI, which stands for General Infantry, or ordinary soldier. In 1965, some people volunteered as GIs in the Vietnam War because they were **patriotic** and wanted to fight for their country. Others signed up because they were keen to leave school or had no job – being in the military would give them a decent wage, skills, and a chance to travel. Most volunteers were men but some were women. Around 11,000 American women volunteered, and 9 out of 10 of these were nurses.

> *When I first went into the armed services, I felt like it was the thing to do. A lot of people were going and a lot of people were leaving school to go. It was an accepted way of growing up.*

Sergeant Eddie Viers, US army

However, the country needed thousands more recruits on the ground in Vietnam in a hurry, so the government started to **draft** people to fight in 1965. The government kept a list of male US residents who were eligible for the draft. To qualify, they had to be over 18 and not perform one of several jobs considered essential for the country, such as farmers, firefighters, and science teachers.

HISTORY DETECTIVES: WHAT IS RESEARCH?

How do we know so much about the Vietnam War? The answer is research. There is a vast amount of information available about almost any topic on the internet, in books, on TV and radio, and other sources. The important thing is to work out what you need to know in addition to what you already know. Then you avoid wasting time or losing focus on non-essential information. Remember the acronym KWL: what I **K**now, what I **W**ant to know, what I have **L**earned.

LYNDON JOHNSON
1908–1973
BORN: Stonewall, Texas, USA

ROLE: Became US president in November 1963 after John F. Kennedy's assassination, and was elected with a large majority in 1964. He was responsible for passing major **civil rights** laws (increasing equality for black Americans) in the early 1960s. Johnson committed the United States to war in Vietnam and drafted thousands of men to fight. As a result, he became a focus for anti-war protests and did not seek re-election in 1968.

Did You Know?

Johnson was famous for giving long, well-informed rants at his opponents with his face up close. The rants were called "The Treatment!"

TRAINING

The people drafted were given physical and mental tests to see if they could become soldiers. New recruits were then sent to camps for basic training from 5 a.m. to 10 p.m. for around two months. This included running and walking while carrying heavy gear, how to behave with officers, and how to stab with a bayonet or fire a rifle. After basic training, most GIs had further training and learnt particular skills such as using tanks and other artillery.

FIGHTING IN VIETNAM

The Vietnam War was a new kind of war for US troops. Some battles were against units of full-time PAVN, which received some military supplies from the USSR and China. In many encounters, GIs were fighting small groups of local Vietcong. The Vietcong often wore clothing similar to those of local villagers rather than uniforms, so this enemy was difficult to identify. They were also expert at staying hidden in the forest.

CONTROVERSIAL WEAPONS

The US military had a massive arsenal of weapons, including B-52 bombers that could drop 30 tonnes of bombs on each raid and highly manoeuvrable Bell Huey helicopters to land and **evacuate** troops. Some of the weapons were controversial. A **chemical weapon** called **Agent Orange** was dropped from planes onto forests to kill the leaves of plants and prevent the Vietcong hiding there. They also used **napalm**, which is a thick, sticky chemical containing fuel that burnt anything it stuck to, from people to village buildings. These chemical weapons were also used to destroy the enemies' food source.

▼ A napalm bomb dropped by a US Air Force plane explodes on a rural Vietnamese village.

The Vietcong often made surprise attacks on supply lines, patrols, and camps. This was guerrilla warfare. They often ambushed GIs using lethal homemade **booby traps** set off by trip wires. The explosives they used to make these were sometimes from unexploded US bombs that they found.

Both the PAVN and the Vietcong built extensive networks of underground tunnels through the country, linking hidden bases safe from overhead bombing. They moved around through the tunnels unnoticed by the US and South Vietnamese forces. In addition, GIs were fighting in hot and damp tropical forest conditions. Sergeant Eddie Viers recalls what it was like:

Vietnam was like hell without fire. We slept on the ground, and you either burned up in the sunshine or froze to death in the rain... The insects were horrible... They gave us insect repellent, but it seemed to me like it just attracted them ... You had to be extremely careful in the jungle for booby traps... There were bamboo [spear] pits, snake pits, ... [land]mines, sticks that would set off artillery rounds and kill a whole group of people, traps that would slice people in half, and that's just to name a few.

HISTORY DETECTIVES:
PRIMARY AND SECONDARY SOURCES

Primary sources are original, first-hand accounts of events. They include transcripts of conversations and speeches, documents such as reports and correspondence, newspaper articles, letters, diaries, photos, and films about events at or around the time they happened.

Secondary sources are created by people who were not there. They often express an opinion or argument about past events. These sources are more commonly available, for example schoolbooks, biographies, and historical films. Use secondary sources to organize your research, but look at primary sources to help bring your research alive and understand how people felt at the time.

WHY DID PEOPLE START TO PROTEST AGAINST THE WAR?

In the early 1960s, many Americans were aware of the threat of communism but few knew much about the Vietnam War. However, some protesting voices were gradually being heard. Some were **pacifists** who opposed all wars, such as Bertrand Russell, the British philosopher, author, and anti-war campaigner. In April 1963, the *New York Times* printed a letter to the editor written by Russell. In it, he accused the US government of "conducting a war of annihilation in Vietnam" in order to suppress communism.

Russell went on to name and shame the United States because "…the war which is being conducted is an **atrocity**. Napalm jelly gasoline is being used against whole villages without warning. Chemical warfare is employed for the purpose of destroying crops and livestock and to starve the population." His letter was an early public criticism of the Vietnam War. Russell set up the Bertrand Russell Peace Foundation that collected evidence that the US government was committing war crimes.

▼ A US Air Force plane sprays Agent Orange onto Vietnamese forest.

BURNING PROTESTS

In 1963, Thich Quang Duc, a Buddhist monk in Vietnam, set himself on fire and died. This was in protest against the cruel South Vietnamese leadership and crackdowns on the monks' activities. Photos and reports about this extreme protest spread worldwide. Two years later, Norman Morrison felt so desperate about the violence his country was inflicting on innocent Vietnamese that he too burnt himself to death on a Washington street below the office of US Secretary of Defense, Robert McNamara.

Other early protesters were those who believed that a better way to stop communism was to encourage better democratic government than the cruel regime offered by the South Vietnamese at that time. These included politicians such as Mike Mansfield. Other reasons for protest were that fighting a war was too expensive at a time when many Americans had little money and few work opportunities, and also that the United States had no obvious economic or other interests in Vietnam.

WHO IN HISTORY

MIKE MANSFIELD
1903–2001

BORN: Brooklyn, New York, USA

ROLE: Mansfield was a US Senator who supported the South Vietnamese regime in the 1950s, but who changed his mind after visiting Vietnam in 1962. He was the first major American politician to question US policy in Vietnam, saying to President John F. Kennedy that the South Vietnamese government had wasted the $2 billion spent there.

Did You Know?

Mansfield was called China Mike because of his knowledge of Asian culture and language, and his calls for better US–Asia relations.

PROTESTS GROW

The first large-scale demonstrations against the war took place in New York in May 1964. Up to 1,000 students marched through Times Square to the United Nations headquarters to protest against US intervention in Vietnam. The organizers said that the protests that year were: "A start, but nowhere near enough. Nowhere near enough because very few students even knew about the war … or what they could do about it. Now thousands know the nature of the war in Vietnam."

In other 1964 protests, popular folk singers, including Joan Baez and Pete Seeger, gave their support to the anti-war protesters by singing songs with anti-war themes such as "Where Have All the Flowers Gone?". This persuaded some people to join the protests. Others protested after hearing and seeing more news and images from the war, such as the large-scale destruction of Vietnam by increased bombing from 1965 onwards.
In 1965, President Johnson gave a speech to explain why the United States needed to help South Vietnam. Read the speech on: www.lbjlib.utexas.edu/johnson/archives.hom/speeches.hom/650407.asp.

▼ Growing numbers of Americans opposed the war and the expectation that they would die for a cause they did not believe in. A demonstrator at this 1967 rally at the Pentagon (see page 15) holds up an image of President Johnson.

WAR MYTHS

There are many myths about the Vietnam War that are repeated in many sources, but are probably not true. Here are a few:

Myth: The average age of troops was 19
Fact: Official figures suggest it was closer to 23, although some GIs were as young as 16

Myth: Most soldiers fighting in Vietnam were drafted and therefore had no choice
Fact: Official figures suggest that around 70 per cent of GIs were volunteers

1967

In 1967, civil rights leader Martin Luther King Jr made a major speech to church leaders, encouraging them to join and promote protests against the Vietnam War. He said: "We must move past indecision to action. We must find new ways to speak for peace in Vietnam and justice throughout the developing world – a world that borders on our doors."

One reason was that he saw a link between the Vietnam War and civil rights not only for the Vietnamese, but also for black Americans. King was concerned by the poor living conditions and lack of job opportunities for many black Americans in large cities. He concluded that high military spending on the Vietnam War meant the government was spending less on improving lives in the United States. King was also aware of the fact that many poor black American men had signed up to join the army, as they had few other job options and were dying in significant numbers at the start of the war.

King's speech helped increase black American involvement in protests and was one reason why marches were getting bigger. Around 100,000 people took part in a major march on Washington in October 1967, to surround the Pentagon. This is a hundred times the number who protested in 1964 in New York City. Bill Ramsey was a 19-year-old student: "This was my first demonstration of any kind... I was among those who reached the steps of the Pentagon first."

WHAT DID STUDENTS DO TO PROTEST?

On the afternoon of 4 May 1970, angry students at Kent State University, Ohio, were protesting against a change in the Vietnam War. The US government had announced that it was invading neighbouring Cambodia and needed more students to join the army. Some students set fire to a university building and prevented firefighters from putting it out. Larry Shafer was one of 1,000 armed National Guardsmen sent to the campus to break up a rally: "You don't send people into a situation like that with the heavy armament that we had. We were combat troops. They were not sending us into a war zone…"

The students chased after the Guardsmen. A student with his hand behind his back approached Shafer: "I felt I was in immediate danger, not knowing whether he had a weapon or a rock." He fired a shot into the stomach of the student, 18-year-old Joseph Lewis. Lewis survived, but other students were not so lucky when other panicked Guardsmen fired. Four students died and nine were injured, one so badly that he spent the rest of his life in a wheelchair.

▼ These students are fleeing the shots of the National Guard at Kent State University in May 1970.

STUDENT OPPOSITION

The events at Kent State were amongst the most notorious of Vietnam War protests. Images showing students killed by armed troops on US soil shocked the nation. However, student Vietnam War protests had been taking place on campuses from around 1964. Why did these young people feel so strongly about what was happening in Vietnam?

WHO IN HISTORY

JAMES A. RHODES
1909–2001
BORN: Coalton, Ohio, USA

ROLE: Rhodes was Republican Governor of Ohio four times. In 1970, he ordered in the Ohio National Guard to Kent State University to stop the protests. He said: *"They're the worst type of people that we harbor in America."*

Did You Know?

Rhodes dropped out of college to open a restaurant called Jim's Place.

HISTORY DETECTIVES: TIMELINES

Timelines help establish the order of events in a period of history. You can organize information by decade and year or month, week, and day.

1 May:	Students at Kent State demonstrate against military action in Cambodia. National Guard are sent in.
2 May:	An army recruitment centre is set on fire. Guards use rubber bullets and tear gas to disperse the crowd.
3 May:	State declares a state of emergency at Kent State; rising tension between Guards and protestors.
4 May:	Guards fire tear gas, retreat, and fire on protestors with live bullets. University is closed.

AT UNIVERSITY

For some students, going to university was their first time away from home and one of the first opportunities to make choices about their beliefs. Others had taken part in the civil rights movement of the early 1960s. Many had little knowledge of Vietnam, but some soon began to question military escalation once the Vietnam War began. David, a student at Columbia University, questioned whether the Gulf of Tonkin incident had actually happened. He wondered if it had been made up to justify existing plans to go to war: "At the time, the handful of us who knew something about Vietnam were exceedingly sceptical. Why would a little boat attack a destroyer?... We thought the incident was probably a deliberate provocation; for questioning our government's version, we were considered 'the lunatic fringe'."

who has a better right to oppose the war?

student mobilization committee to end the war in vietnam

▲ This poster was produced by a student group in 1969. Its message was that everyone, from soldiers to peace protestors (symbolized by the dove), had the right to protest the Vietnam War.

Some had great sympathy for the North Vietnamese, who they believed were being bullied by the United States. Of course, other students were right behind the war and were angry that some students would want to protest against it. They showed this anger in different ways such as disowning protesters. Student Bill Ramsey recalled in 1967: "I was interviewed by the school paper, as the first student to participate in an anti-war march. My fraternity brothers harassed me and eventually expelled me from the 'brotherhood'."

STUDENT GROUPS

A number of organizations led student anti-war protests. One of the main groups was Students for a Democratic Society (SDS), founded in 1960. SDS grew rapidly after the United States went to war in Vietnam. David Gilbert recalls organizing an SDS demonstration:

> [I]t ... dawned on me that no matter how big this demonstration turned out to be, it wouldn't end the war; that was going to take a much more developed movement. So we decided beforehand to plan our next ... meetings and events ... so that we could pass out flyers to everyone on the buses ... and encourage people to participate.

By early 1966, there were 10,000 members on 150 university campuses. SDS organizers produced pamphlets and badges to sell to students, put up posters, and organized talks and marches. They sent representatives to witness the destruction caused by the United States in Vietnam, paid for students to get to marches, and at protests they sometimes waved PAVN flags.

> Most of us grew up thinking that the United States was a strong but humble nation that ... respected the integrity of other nations and other systems; and that engaged in wars only as a last resort... [But] The incredible war in Vietnam has provided the razor, the terrifying sharp cutting edge that has finally severed the last vestige of illusion that morality and democracy are the guiding principles of American foreign policy ... the United States may well be the greatest threat to peace in the world today.
> Paul Potter, SDS President, 1965

HOW DID STUDENTS PROTEST?

Some students protested violently by shouting, pushing, and throwing things at police and soldiers. However, most students protested non-violently by marching, giving out leaflets, and disrupting studies. In 1968, SDS became widely known when students at Columbia University occupied student buildings and almost completely stopped any teaching and study at the university until police arrived. Newspaper and TV coverage publicized their action. Students would often sit or lie on the floor to make removing them from occupied buildings more difficult. Protests were sometimes symbolic and drew lots of attention. In a 1969 protest in Central Park, New York, around 10,000 students lay down on the grass and released 10,000 black balloons to represent GIs killed in Vietnam since President Nixon was elected.

LEARNING ABOUT THE WAR

Professors and other academics began to use **teach-ins** to protest against the Vietnam War. In March 1965, 23 professors at the University of Michigan proposed a one-day strike during which they would refuse to take classes and instead teach interested students about what was really happening in Vietnam. State authorities threatened to sack the professors if they did. So the academics decided upon a teach-in from 8 p.m. until 8 a.m. The authorities gave permission to use lecture halls and other facilities.

◀ These students have just held a 13-hour sit-in to protest against the war at a university campus building in Colorado, USA in 1972.

At the teach-in, students heard lectures from experts on the war, such as former State Department advisor Robert Browne who told the crowd that the war was unwinnable owing to the nature of the terrain. They debated issues with their professors. One of the speakers, Arthur Waskow, said: "This teach-in is in the true spirit of a university where students and faculty learn from each other." Teach-ins spread to other universities and many students became highly informed about the war. The involvement of professors also gave respectability to Vietnam War protests that had previously been associated only with radical students.

> It was real exciting to stay up all night and listen to people talk about Vietnam. A whole different picture emerged from what we were getting from the mainstream media and the government... One of the things that drove the teach-in back in the late 1960s was that ... there were students who had been drafted and sent to the war in Vietnam. So you wake up one day and say, where is Bob and where is Joe?

Bunyan Bryant, 2001 (present at the teach-in in 1965)

WHERE WERE YOUR RELATIVES?

Do you have any grandparents or other relatives who were at university in the late 1960s and 1970s? What are their recollections of anti-war protests at that time? Did they take part? Do they have any primary sources such as photos, leaflets, and badges?

TEACH-INS ON TV

The Michigan University Television Center recorded several student protests on film in the 1960s and 70s, including the first teach-in. You can view this at http://ummedia10.rs.itd.umich.edu/flash/bentley/bhlflash.html?dep=bentley&file=851831/AF/851831-AF190-a.flv. Although some of the film is poor quality and sound is not always clear, it gives an idea of the feelings of the people involved including professors Eric Wolfe and William Gamson.

BURNING DRAFT CARDS

Many important politicians, business leaders, and other middle class, affluent people in America had studied at universities when they were younger. Students were not called up while studying partly in an effort to prevent losing support for the war amongst this group of people. However, the draft loomed in the near future for young male students and some resented not having the choice of whether to fight or not. One form of protest for people who were to be called up was to damage their draft cards. President Johnson signed a law in August 1965 making this illegal and punishable by a $1,000 fine and up to five years in prison.

But public burning of draft cards became a memorable method of protesting. The first card burner at a university was an Iowa student called Stephen Lynn Smith. He burnt his card in October 1965 at a weekly open-mic session in the Iowa Memorial Union. While some audience members cheered, others jeered. Smith said: "I do not feel that five years of my life are too much to give to say that this law is wrong."

▼ The simple act of burning a draft card had great significance as a protest during the Vietnam War.

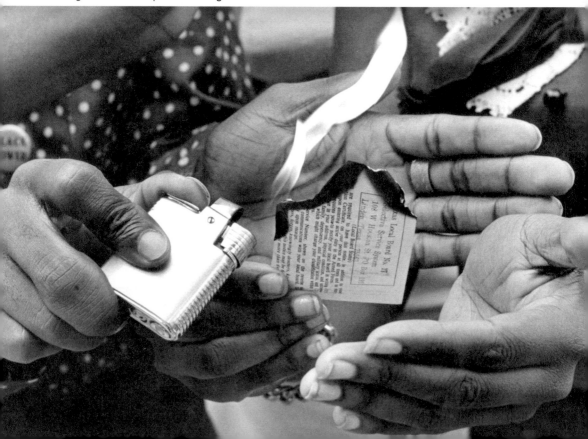

TURNING POINT: 1970

Three events increased student and other protests against the war:

1. Cambodia: in 1970, revelations came to light that Nixon had started bombing Cambodia in secret in 1969. Plans to send in troops to Cambodia were also announced. This incensed students, as they believed Cambodia was an innocent country not involved in the war.

2. Changes to the draft: the government drafted a further 150,000 students to fight straight away rather than wait until after their courses finished.

3. Kent State and Jackson State: two weeks after Kent State, two students were killed and twelve injured by police forces who opened fire on anti-war demonstrators at Jackson State University, Mississippi. After these events, colleges and universities across the United States closed for the remainder of the academic year in fear of violent protests on their campuses.

The following day's newspapers reported that Smith's father was unsympathetic and highly critical of his son's action. A day later, government agents arrested Smith at his home and he was sentenced to three years' **probation**.

DRAFT CHANGE

Some people said they were conscientious objectors who would not fight on principle; other people left the country. By 1969, draft refusal and burning cards was increasing across campuses. The new president, Richard Nixon, had changed the law so that students could now not put off their draft until after their courses had finished. In all, around half a million students refused the draft during the Vietnam War. Students were not the only ones to refuse the draft, however. In 1972, there were more refusers than people actually drafted, and the law courts of cities across the nation had backlogs of legal cases.

WHY DID SOLDIERS PROTEST?

In 2011, an expert on the Vietnam War, Robert Destatte, was reading an article on a Vietnamese website when he noticed that one writer mentioned unsent letters from a GI. Destatte got in touch with the writer and this led to him discovering letters written by Sergeant Steve Flaherty, who had been killed in 1969.

Flaherty was born in Japan but was adopted and moved to the United States when he was nine. He had a baseball scholarship at university but chose instead to enlist. The letters had been taken from his clothing before he was buried, and had been kept in a white envelope for around 43 years until Destatte got hold of them. They were finally returned to Flaherty's family in 2012, when the US and Vietnamese governments officially exchanged war **artefacts**. Steve's family now knew where his body had been buried and what he had been thinking and wanting to say to them around the time of his death. Here is an excerpt from a letter to a friend:

> We have been in a fierce fight with [the Vietcong]. We took in lots of casualties and death. It has been trying days for me and my men. We dragged more bodies of dead and wounded than I can ever want to forget… Thank you for your sweet card. It made my miserable day a much better one but I don't think I will ever forget the bloody fight we are having. I felt bullets going past me. I have never been so scared in my life.

FAR FROM HOME

Letters such as Flaherty's are proof that primary sources which help us understand past events are constantly being found. They also confirm that many GIs in Vietnam were having a very tough time. Like all soldiers at war, they were lonely, scared, sometimes bored, and shocked by the things they had seen and done. However, GIs had the added stress of not only being in an unfamiliar place fighting a hidden enemy, but also hearing news from home about the growing anti-war protests. Many felt confused about what they were doing in Vietnam and felt isolated from their own country.

PROTEST FROM THE DEAD

Keith Franklin was killed in action on 12 May 1970, and a letter was found on him:

> *The question is whether or not my death has been in vain. The answer is yes. The war that has taken my life and many thousands before me is immoral, unlawful and an atrocity... I had no choice as to my fate. It was predetermined by the warmongering hypocrites in Washington. As I lie dead, please grant my last request. Help me inform the American people, the silent majority who have not yet voiced their opinions.*

▼ Letters home from GIs are not only important primary sources about the war in general, but also provide us with evidence of a growing awareness amongst troops of anti-war feelings in their country.

CASUALTIES OF WAR

Soldiers also felt they wanted to protest against the war because of the high casualty rate they saw. Over 300,000 American soldiers were wounded in action and a quarter of these were disabled as a result. The booby traps and mines used by the Vietcong caused a large number of lower body injuries. Soldiers were likely to survive such injuries in the Vietnam War because of speedy evacuation from the battlefield by helicopter. However, many suffered amputations, especially of legs. Over 58,000 American fighters died during the war, although about one-sixth of these died accidentally or as a result of illness. Body counts were less accurate for Vietnamese soldiers. However, a study in 1995 estimated that 1 million Vietnamese were killed in the war from 1965 to 1975.

TURNING POINT: 1968

Deadliest year: Over 16,000 US troops killed, the highest year total of the war

Tet Offensive: Massive co-ordinated North Vietnamese attacks on cities and towns in South Vietnam, including Saigon, killed tens of thousands of Vietnamese and over 1,700 US troops. Americans realized that they were nowhere near the end of the war.

Cost: US war spending was estimated at US$66 million dollars a day

▼ The bodies of US soldiers killed in action in Vietnam are loaded on a transport plane for return to the United States.

HISTORY DETECTIVES:
QUESTIONING PRIMARY SOURCES

Not all primary sources are what they seem, and part of the job of any researcher is to question them. It is also important to watch out for bias in any sources you use. Taking primary sources at face value may distort the truth or present only one side of the story.

Below is a good example of how a primary source may be misleading. Some soldiers in Vietnam wrote about horrors that they had merely imagined, possibly to make people at home proud or to reflect the dangerous situation they were in. Paul O'Connell wrote a letter to his parents, dated 16 December 1968, in which he said:

Well, three days ago we were chopper'd [transported by helicopter] onto Hill 500 where we were met by an NVA battalion. I need not say more except I escaped without a scratch, but I'm still shaking. I hope I never have to see a dead Marine again. I lost my best buddy from Indiana, and my other buddy ... lost his legs from his knees down.

However, after O'Connell re-read the letter in 1996, he said:

The expectations, the thoughts of dying or being maimed were as much a killer as actually being killed. As for my friend from Indiana ... he didn't die. No one got hit. No one lost from the knees down. The truth of the matter ... nothing happened other than we made a combat assault upon Hill 500 ... fixed to kill everything that got in our way, fixed to die if we had to; and yet, nothing happened.

Examples like this illustrate why it is good to have several sources to corroborate facts.

HORRORS OF WAR

In spring 1968, a US soldier called Ron Ridenhour heard about a massacre carried out by US troops in a hamlet called My Lai. Lieutenant William Calley had been ordered to lead his unit, Charlie Company, into My Lai to search for Vietcong. They found no Vietcong but rounded up and murdered over 500 civilians. Officers tried to cover up the massacre to avoid a scandal. Ridenhour wrote letters to the president, the Pentagon, and several politicians. One said: "Exactly what did, in fact, occur in the village … I do not know for certain, but … if you and I … believe in the principles, of justice and the equality of every man, … then we must press forward a widespread and public investigation of this matter."

No investigation followed so Ridenhour gave an interview to journalist Seymour Hersh who went public with the story in November 1969. The story forced a US Army investigation that ended with Calley being sent to prison. None of his men were punished.

▼ A film crew records the return of GIs from the invasion of Cambodia in 1970. The reception for US troops was not always so pleasant after the events of My Lai.

PUBLIC VIEWS OF GIS

My Lai had a massive impact on public perception of GIs in the United States. Some people started believing that all soldiers were unnecessarily brutal – and even murderers. Machine-gunner Terry Tople was injured in action in Vietnam and remembers his treatment on returning home:

> I came out on a stretcher at Travis Air Force Base in California, and I got stuff thrown at me, rotten eggs, tomatoes. All of us coming off that airplane were wounded, and they were throwing stuff at us... They were yelling at us. I can refer back to when the World War II people came home and they were heroes. When we came home we ... felt like we were the enemy. That really hurt.

Many soldiers thought such public treatment was desperately unfair and blamed leaders of the anti-war movement and the press for turning the public against them. Others wondered how many more cover-ups of massacres such as My Lai had happened. These soldiers blamed their country for exposing them to the horrors of war and making them behave cruelly as a result.

> Before I went over there I was stupid and didn't pay much attention to what was going on politically ... at home. But I remember coming home and people asking stuff like how many babies you killed ... I became an anti-war activist, so-to-speak, and I was very much so against the war.

Gary Caroll, GI speaking in 2005

HISTORY DETECTIVES: CONFLICTING SOURCES

Some primary sources about the same topics can put across different opinions. The first newspaper reports were based on official US military reports and described My Lai as a military victory in which the United States had killed 128 Vietcong with a small number of civilian casualties. After Ridenhour's efforts, a US Congress investigation, and confessions by eyewitnesses, newspaper reports described the troop action as murder and massacre.

HOW DID SOLDIERS PROTEST?

Soldiers protested in a variety of ways. Some refused to carry out their duty. In June 1965, Lieutenant Richard Steinke refused to board an aircraft taking him to fight in a remote Vietnamese village. He said, "The Vietnamese war is not worth a single American life." In 1967, an army doctor refused to teach Special Forces troops called Green Berets because he claimed they were "murderers of women and children". Such military personnel faced **court-martial** for refusing to do their duty and risked being imprisoned as well as being thrown out of the military.

Other soldiers burned or destroyed official military material just as students had burned draft cards. Some threw away medals given to them by their government for bravery while fighting. Many people were shocked that soldiers should reject medals received for serving their country and sometimes for trying to protect or save other soldiers in battle. Some soldiers were rejected by their families as a result of returning their medals.

> *My parents told me that if I really did come down here and turn in my medals, they never wanted anything more to do with me. That's not an easy thing to take. I still love my parents. My wife doesn't understand what happened to me when I came home from Nam [Vietnam]. She said she would divorce me if I came down here because she wanted my medals for our son to see when he grew up.*

Ron Ferrizzi, after disowning his Silver Star and Purple Heart medals, which had been awarded for gallantry and bravery, and for being wounded in action

DESERTING

During the Vietnam War, over half a million members of the US armed forces deserted. This means abandoning their post or duty to fight without permission and with no intention of returning. In 1971, 177 out of every 1,000 American soldiers were officially listed as "absent without leave". Thousands left the country and many of these chose Canada or places in Western Europe such as France, Sweden, and the Netherlands. Some even took sanctuary in US churches where they were protected by anti-war sympathizers until their eventual arrest.

▲ From left to right: the Silver Star, the Bronze Star, and the Purple Heart. These are some of the most important military decorations given to US troops for bravery in combat in Vietnam.

LEARNING MORE

Soldiers returning from Vietnam wanted to know more about the war and why people were protesting – but not the official military versions. Some went to GI coffeehouses around the country where soldiers could get coffee and doughnuts, find anti-war literature, and talk freely with others. Others read unofficial newspapers produced at military bases such as *About Face* in Los Angeles and *Fed Up!* in Tacoma, Washington. These printed anti-war articles, gave news about the harassment of GIs, and provided practical advice on the legal rights of servicemen in refusing to serve.

VIETNAM VETERANS TOGETHER

At a peace demonstration in New York City in April 1967, a group of six soldiers marched under the banner "Vietnam **Veterans** Against the War". This was the first activity of a new protest group of the same name, representing veterans or soldiers who had fought for their country. They were protesting against the very war they had fought in.

The VVAW steadily grew in size as more veterans protested. In 1970, the VVAW had 600 members but by 1971, it had many thousands. One reason was the Winter Soldier Investigation held to publicize war crimes sanctioned and ordered by the military in Vietnam. One hundred veterans testified about what they had seen or taken part in during active duty. Seven times this number of veterans came to listen. The investigation not only encouraged many more veterans to join VVAW, but also sparked many military investigations into events. Find out more about the Winter Soldier Investigation at: www2.iath.virginia.edu/sixties/HTML_docs/Resources/ Primary/Winter_Soldier/WS_entry.html.

▼ These Vietnam War veterans are demonstrating together with thousands of other peace protestors in the Mall, Washington, DC in the early 1970s.

WHO IN HISTORY

RON KOVIC
1946
BORN: Ladysmith, Wisconsin, USA

ROLE: Kovic is a famous Vietnam veteran protester active in VVAW. Son of US Navy parents, Kovic wanted to be a military hero. On his second **tour of duty** in 1968, he was paralysed from the chest down after being shot. The poor military hospital conditions he experienced in the United States when he returned, and the Kent State killings, made him question why he had gone to Vietnam.

Did You Know?

Kovic interrupted Nixon's acceptance speech at the Republican National Convention saying, "I gave America my all, and the leaders of this government threw me and others away to rot in their VA hospitals. What's happening in Vietnam is a crime against humanity."

TO WASHINGTON

A second reason for VVAW's popularity was its march on Washington in 1971, which involved around 1,000 veterans. Many were on crutches or in wheelchairs, having left the service when disabled. The veterans entered the US Senate and protested that the war was illegal. One veteran, John Kerry, gave evidence from the Winter Soldier Investigation to the Senate:

Several months ago ... we had an investigation at which over 150 honorably discharged, and many very highly decorated, veterans testified to war crimes committed in South-East Asia. These were not isolated incidents but crimes committed on a day to day basis with a full awareness of officers at all levels of command.

PENTAGON PAPERS

In mid-1971, a series of reports were published in the *New York Times* that shocked the country. They were based on the Pentagon Papers, a secret Department of Defense study of US political and military involvement in Vietnam (1945–1967). The Papers stated that even before the United States officially became involved, they had repeatedly given military aid to South Vietnam and made the conflict with North Vietnam worse. Before the publication of the Papers, the US public had largely thought that the United States went to war to help peaceful South Vietnam avoid takeover by hostile North Vietnam.

▲ The US government tried to stop the *New York Times* from publishing further extracts of the Pentagon Papers, as leaked by Daniel Ellsberg.

Daniel Ellsberg, an ex-marine corps officer working as an analyst in the Pentagon, leaked the papers. He had helped prepare the report as part of the team planning the war. They had expected the United States to win the war. However, by 1969 Ellsberg had concluded that the Vietnam War was unwinnable.

Ellsberg thought the public should know what was in the Pentagon Papers, but he was afraid of taking personal risk to reveal the truth. But then he heard a tearful speech by Randy Kehler, who was about to go to prison for refusing the draft.

Kehler described the importance of doing the right thing by joining the anti-war movement and:

> finding a community of people for the first time that not only ... were committed to each other, but ... committed to something larger than themselves, something more noble, more ideal than anything I had been involved in after 22 years. I'm very excited that I'll be invited to join [other draft resisters in prison] very soon.

Ellsberg said, "If I hadn't met Randy Kehler it wouldn't have occurred to me to copy [the Pentagon Papers]. His actions spoke to me as no mere words would have done."

Ellsberg knew his government career was over when he made the papers public. The US government tried in vain to block publication in the newspaper saying that it could harm national security; they also tried unsuccessfully to get Ellsberg sent to prison. But the revelations in the Pentagon Papers made many more people want to protest against the Vietnam War, especially as they had been leaked by a senior US military employee. See the Pentagon Papers at: www.archives.gov/research/pentagon-papers.

HISTORY DETECTIVES:
HANDS-ON RESEARCH

On internet web pages and in books you may often see images or transcripts of primary sources. Actually having first-hand experience of primary sources makes a difference in helping to imagine the past. So, for example, visiting the Vietnam Veterans Memorial to dead soldiers in Washington, DC and seeing the soldiers' ages and names, or handling purple heart medals or letters home in an archive can bring a subject alive.

WHO TOLD THE WORLD ABOUT THE WAR?

In June 1972, a photograph that shocked people all around the world appeared in newspapers. It showed children running from a Vietcong-occupied village just after a napalm airstrike by US aeroplanes. The girl in the centre is naked, having ripped off her clothes to try to stop her skin from burning. Nick Ut took the photo and sent the film back to the Saigon office of the AP picture agency he worked for, run by Horst Faas. Here, photo editors examined the images to see which ones should be sent to the New York office for sale to newspapers. In 2012, Nick Ut said:

> *A couple of AP photo editors rejected the picture because the girl was nude. When Faas came back from lunch ... he asked about it. Why was it still here? He convinced the editors that the photo needed to be sent, just as it was. So the "Napalm Girl" picture was transmitted to AP New York headquarters and the rest of the world. It became the Pulitzer Prize-winning photo for News that year.*

▼ Nick Ut's photo captured the horrific moment when children, including Kim Phuc Phan Thi (centre), flee a napalm attack on their village in 1972.

WHO IN HISTORY

HORST FAAS
1933–2012
BORN: Berlin, Germany

ROLE: Faas was a famous war photographer and ran the Associated Press picture agency. He recruited and trained other photographers and made available important images of the Vietnam War. He photographed at the frontline of conflicts worldwide, including in Congo, Bangladesh, Algeria, and Vietnam.

Did You Know?

Horst Faas learnt English while playing as drummer in a jazz band with black American soldiers in Munich at the end of World War II.

WAR REPORTING

During the Vietnam War, newspaper reporters, photographers, and television crews were common in combat zones. They took risks and suffered many of the same hardships as the soldiers and personnel they were covering. The US military gave the press freedom of access to document the events of the war. The military also collected their own visual record of operations, equipment, and personnel in the war through teams of military photographers. Some images from the war, such as Nick Ut's, became famous. Vietnam War protesters used them as primary source evidence of why the war should be stopped.

[Images] did not show winners and losers. They showed soldiers – often teenagers – coping as best they could with unrelenting heat and humidity, heavy packs, heavy guns, and an invisible enemy whose mines, booby traps, and snipers could cut life short without a moment's warning.

C. Douglas Elliott, *Vietnam: Images from Combat Photographers*, 1994

ICONIC IMAGES

Iconic images are images that represent something more than just the events they are depicting. In the case of memorable Vietnam War images, they are iconic because they trigger emotions of outrage and sadness in the viewer. They do this because they show innocent or powerless people suffering. In Nick Ut's image, the fact that the girl is naked makes her appear very vulnerable, and our sense of outrage is increased by the soldier calmly walking behind the children and not helping them out.

Another iconic image of the war was taken by Eddie Adams. He was in Saigon in 1968 during the Tet Offensive (see page 26), a period of co-ordinated attack on Saigon and other towns by PAVN and NLF forces. In the chaos, he saw South Vietnamese soldiers capturing a Vietcong prisoner and their General Loan taking out his pistol:

> I raised the camera thinking he was going to threaten him. I took a picture. That was the instant he shot him. I had no idea it was going to happen. He put the pistol back in his pocket and walked over to us and said, "He killed many of my men and many of your people."

▼ A tragic instant in the Vietnam War became a long-lasting iconic image about the brutality and morality of the conflict.

HISTORY DETECTIVES:
INTERPRETING A PHOTO

Have you heard the expression "Every picture tells a story"? Unlike a piece of writing, such as a letter or diary, a photograph appears to be objective or unbiased because it is showing what someone has seen through a camera lens. But like any primary source, no photo is completely unbiased. A photographer will have chosen what to show and what to leave out. Newspaper or magazine workers may have cropped or digitally adjusted pictures to show something that supports a news story. Take care in researching photos. Check the subject and content and find out about its context: What was the photographer's intention? Was he or she hired for a particular purpose? Did he or she know the subject?

The prisoner was actually a local NLF leader who had killed the family of one of Loan's friends and gunned down a Saigon policeman. The picture became famous instantly. However, to US war protesters the image did not seem to show punishment for a crime but rather the execution of a defenceless citizen by the South Vietnamese military. It made people question why the United States were helping a regime that could be so cruel. Shooting an unarmed person, even in war, cannot be justified. But the photo does demonstrate how the context of the incident and the public perception of it are different. Eddie Adams wrote in 1998:

> *The general killed the Viet Cong; I killed the general with my camera. Still photographs are the most powerful weapon in the world. People believe them, but photographs do lie, even without manipulation. They are only half-truths... What the photograph didn't say was, "What would you do if you were the general at that time and place on that hot day, and you caught the so-called bad guy after he blew away one, two or three American soldiers?" The guy was a hero.*

WAR IN THE LIVING ROOM

The Vietnam War is sometimes known as the "living room war" because the American public got a lot of their news about it from the TV in their front rooms. By the early 1970s, 48 per cent of people in a survey said they trusted TV to get the truth compared with just 21 per cent for newspapers. Film and reports of destruction could bring the horror of war home to viewers. In 1965, the correspondent Morley Safer produced a broadcast that showed the cruelty of US troops in Vietnam in burning the village of Cam Ne on a search-and-destroy mission. In 2003, Safer said:

Think About This

Bringing news home
Today, modern mobile technology and mobile internet networks make it possible for people to take photos, record film, and supply first-hand accounts of events within minutes of them happening. Do you think Vietnam War protests would have grown faster with modern technology? How could social networks help future war protests be more successful?

Cam Ne was a shock, I think. It's hard for me to know exactly, because I was thirteen thousand miles away, with really lousy communication, so I only got the reverberation of the shock. I think [viewers] saw American troops acting in a way people had never seen American troops act before, and couldn't imagine ... this conjured up not America, but some brutal power – Germany, even, in World War II.

But reports like Safer's were not usual. Film of dead or wounded people was rare and battles were usually shown in the distance in the early years of the war. TV networks did not want to put off their viewers with violent scenes. News broadcasts were usually kept upbeat with battle maps, numbers of enemies killed, and film showing American soldiers in action or reporting tales of bravery.

CHANGING REPORTS

On 27 February 1968, millions of Americans tuned into the evening news for the usual round-up of events in the war. There was daily news of many US troops being killed or being forced to retreat. Newsreader Walter Cronkite finished his report saying:

> ...it seems now more certain than ever, that the bloody experience of Vietnam is to end in a stalemate ...it is increasingly clear to this reporter that the only rational way out then will be to negotiate, not as victors, but as an honourable people who lived up to their pledge to defend democracy, and did the best they could.

For Cronkite to say the war was unwinnable mattered because his opinions were respected nationwide. Soon after that, with Tet Offensive casualties rising fast, President Johnson announced he would not seek re-election and that the war would have to change course. TV coverage of the war also started to change. There was more emphasis put on the human costs of war and more reporting of the Vietnam War protests.

▼ A still from Morley Safer's Cam Ne report from 1965, that made many Americans question their troops' mission and purpose in Vietnam.

HOW DID WAR PROTEST BECOME WIDESPREAD?

▲ Jimi Hendrix's powerful performance at Woodstock came to symbolise the 1960s for many people.

The famous Woodstock festival in August 1969 featured the leading rock and folk artists of the day, from Jimi Hendrix to Joan Baez. Around half a million people attended. The peaceful crowd heard lots of music with anti-war messages. A young music journalist at the festival, Billy Altman, recalls Hendrix's guitar playing:

"The Star-Spangled Banner" just filled the air. It just sounded like the Vietnam War … like a firefight … helicopters... He made it sound like everything that was going on in our country, and around the world at that moment... It showed that just because you don't agree with the way things are doesn't mean you are any less of an American.

Hendrix even burned the American flag as part of his act. The performers were spurred on by an audience that mostly believed in peace, love, and an end to the Vietnam War. For many, Woodstock defined a whole generation of young people who questioned and hoped to improve their society.

SPREADING PROTEST

In the late 1960s, several women's protest groups emerged, including Another Mother for Peace. The group was founded in 1967 by mothers concerned that their children would be sent to war when they grew up. The group lobbied government to solve conflicts non-violently, and spread their message, for example, by selling Mother's Day cards with messages of peace.

The anti-war culture spread partly through advertising. Organizers of the Moratorium to End the War in 1969 wanted to attract a big audience, so they produced an advert for the event. Organizer Sam Brown said in 1982:

It was a picture of a father and a son with their arms around each other. The son with hair down to his waist and the father with a crew cut and the cut line under it said "fathers and sons together against the war." I mean everything was designed to appeal to the broadest mass of the American people.

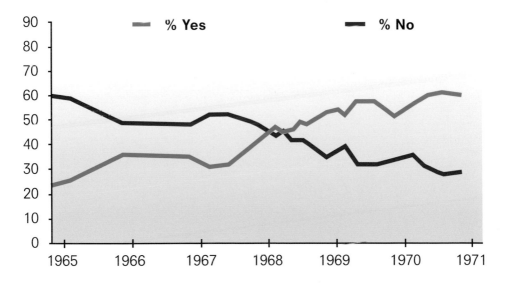

▲ In response to polls asking whether people thought it was a mistake to send US troops to war, about 60% said no in 1965. But the same poll in 1971 revealed that about 60% believed it *was* a mistake. This change was owing to concerns about the war such as the increased draft, reports of atrocities, and costs.

PROTEST SONGS

In the mid-1960s, people were hearing lots of music on radio and television. They were buying over US$1 billion worth of music a year. Songs with an anti-war message were becoming more common. One of the most popular was "I Feel Like I'm Fixin' To Die Rag" by Country Joe and the Fish (1965):

Come on mothers throughout the land,
Pack your boys off to Vietnam.
Come on fathers, don't hesitate,
Send your sons off before it's too late.
You can be the first one on your block
To have your boy come home in a box.

Country Joe and the Fish were skilled at getting crowds singing along to their songs. As lead singer, Joe McDonald, said: "Good protest music must be entertaining or else it is just propaganda."

▼ The anti-war stance of Country Joe and the Fish struck a chord with the public.

Another protest song, Crosby, Stills, Nash, and Young's "Ohio" (1970), was about the Kent State shootings. The song was recorded and released within a month of the event. Other songs were against war in general. Some of the most popular were John Lennon's "Give Peace a Chance" (1969) and Edwin Starr's 1970 soul hit "War":

War, huh, yeah
What is it good for?
Absolutely (nothing), ah, ha, ha, ha

See the words to some more anti-war songs at: www.digitalhistory.uh.edu/learning_history/vietnam/vietnam_music.cfm.

CELEBRITIES

Pop and rock stars were not the only celebrities behind the anti-war movement. The most notable sports celebrity to protest was Muhammad Ali, the world heavyweight boxing champion. In 1966, he refused to be drafted and as a result had his title taken from him, did not fight for three and a half years, and was sentenced to prison. Many people sent Ali threatening letters and criticized him for his stand. The Governor of Maine said that Ali "should be held in utter contempt by every patriotic American". Other celebrity protesters included the actors Henry and Jane Fonda.

WHO IN HISTORY

| JANE FONDA | BORN: New York City, |
| 1937 | New York, USA |

ROLE: Fonda was an actress widely known during the Vietnam War for her protests. After meeting US military deserters, she toured US military bases and GI coffeehouses, meeting soldiers and arguing against the war. She became known as "Hanoi Jane". She was criticized heavily in the United States after visiting North Vietnam and meeting its armed forces.

Did You Know?

Fonda made a popular exercise video in 1982 that sold 17 million copies worldwide.

▲ Women from the "Save Our Sons" organization stand in silent protest against the Vietnam War outside government offices in Sydney, Australia in June 1966.

INTERNATIONAL OPPOSITION

The Vietnam War protests were not just in the United States. The United States wanted its **allies** to help out in the Vietnam War. South Korea, Australia, New Zealand, the Philippines, and Thailand all sent combat troops or supporting forces. The United Kingdom gave no military support but officially approved of US action. Protest in the United Kingdom peaked with clashes outside the US Embassy in London in March and October 1968. See a video of the 1968 anti-war protests in London at: www.britishpathe.com/video/london-riots-anti-vietnam-demonstration-ends-in.

In 1965, a group called Save Our Sons (SOS) was formed by Australian women concerned that their sons would be called up to fight as more troops were sent to Vietnam. One of the founding members of SOS was Joan Coxsedge. She grew up in a working class family in Melbourne with little interest in politics and worked as a commercial artist before getting married and raising three children. When Australia got involved in Vietnam Joan became an active protester with SOS: "…we walked around and around in a sedate circle holding up anti-war placards. No shouting of slogans or [taunting] of opponents, we were warned, although I was sorely tempted to retaliate when a middle-aged man in a business suit sidled up and hissed 'You should all be crucified'."

She and other SOS members were arrested several times for sit-ins and other protests: "I lived in a very conservative area... At that time I was in and out of gaol [prison] and prominently named in the newspapers as a result of various protest actions, so you can imagine how they loved me!"

AUSTRALIAN PUBLIC PROTEST

By the early 1970s, the protest movement was more widespread in Australia. Moratorium rallies were being held in major cities, including Sydney and Melbourne, attracting more than 200,000 people in total. Protesters carried out candlelit processions and church services. The moratoriums involved not only SOS members, draft resisters, and students, but also politicians opposing their government's involvement in the war, church leaders, teachers, and pupils.

> I went on three Moratoriums [moratorium rallies], and took kids from Balwyn High. We made banners in the woodwork room which infuriated other teachers... A lot of the time you were the only person in your family, workplace, or street who opposed the war.

Gary Guest, teacher and moratorium protestor

HISTORY DETECTIVES: THE INTERNET

There are millions of websites out there and some have unreliable information. When you find something that might be useful, you cannot always tell who wrote it and when. One way to evaluate websites is by checking the end of the website address. Sites produced by governments (.gov) or educational organizations (.edu) may be less biased than commercial sites (.com or .net). You could also look for links on the website revealing something about the authors. Was the website written by a respected author or academic? Are there citations to show where the website got its information?

WHAT HAPPENED TO THE PROTESTERS AFTER THE WAR?

During the early 1970s, the United States gradually pulled their troops out of Vietnam, leaving South Vietnamese forces in control of ground operations. However, the United States continued its aerial bombing of North Vietnam. In early 1973, the last of the US troops came home, funding for US combat operations in Vietnam stopped, and the draft ended. US involvement in the war was over and there were far fewer anti-war protests. In Vietnam, the PAVN stepped up attacks on the South and finally took control of the South's capital Saigon in 1975 and unified the country. The longest war of the 20th century, involving the United States, had ended.

VETERANS AFTER THE WAR

Many veterans lost a major focus in their lives when the war ended. Jack Day was a veteran who had been a chaplain at the VVAW protest at Arlington Memorial. He remembers hearing news of the advances of the North Vietnamese on Saigon and place names familiar to him from his tour of duty:

> The rightness or wrongness of what we had done in Vietnam stopped mattering for a while. These were places American lives had been sacrificed to defend, and now they were gone. It was a very upsetting time … of pre-occupation with every bit of news, every detail, as if it were our own lives which were still in danger… It was a time of adrenaline and staying awake late at night and finding it hard to concentrate on the requirements of everyday life. Finally, it was over, and the news stopped, and there was a void, a sort of ache that would last for years.

Many veterans struggled to cope with the return to normal life. Some had trouble sleeping and, if woken suddenly, could become violent. This was because they had been trained to expect and respond to surprise attacks

▲ Veterans of recent wars meet and chat at the
Veteran Center at California State University in 2010.

from the enemy. Some had drug or mental health problems that started in
Vietnam. Even those without such problems were sometimes refused work
by employers who thought that veterans would be unreliable.

POST–TRAUMATIC STRESS DISORDER (PTSD)

On return from war, significant numbers of veterans started to
experience similar mental health problems. These included intense
feelings of guilt, feeling unable to love and trust others, flashbacks
of what they had seen and felt in battle, and fear of loud noises.
Today, such difficulties are called **post-traumatic stress disorder
(PTSD)**, but in the 1970s, doctors called it Post-Vietnam Syndrome.
Veterans with PTSD had little or no support from the government on
their return. However, from 1979 Vet Centers were established where
veterans could get treatment and help with their difficulties.

STORY OF HIS LIFE

Ron Kovic of the VVAW left military hospital after the war ended. His autobiography, *Born on the Fourth of July*, was published in 1976. By chance, Ron met Oliver Stone, a young film director who was also a Vietnam veteran. Stone said that if he ever became famous he would make the film of Ron's book. For the next 10 years, Ron travelled around staying in cheap hotels and on friend's couches, finding it difficult to settle down. Then in 1987, he got an unexpected call from Stone. Stone was now a famous director who had just made a film called *Platoon*, based on his own Vietnam War experiences. Stone said: "Ronnie, I'm ready." After watching *Born on the Fourth of July*, Ron said: "It was an incredible experience. I was looking at myself live through the most difficult periods of my life. I was forced to deal with the reality of the hell that I had lived through in a way that I never dealt with it before." Read interviews of other veterans at openvault.wgbh.org/collections/vietnam-the-vietnam-collection.

INTO MEDICINE

As a teenager, Craig Venter was a war protester. He volunteered for the Navy to avoid the draft in which he would probably have become a frontline soldier in battle. He spent his tour of duty in a naval hospital. With only basic medical training, he had to treat badly injured soldiers because there were not enough doctors.

> *I learned more than any 20-year-old should ever have to about ... sorting those you can salvage from those you cannot do anything for, except ease their pain as they died... [It] transformed me from a young man without direction and purpose into a man driven to understand the very essence of life and to use that understanding to change medicine.*

After the war, Craig studied medicine and then became a scientific researcher into genes. Genes are the chemical codes that control our bodies. Craig became famous in 2000 for identifying all the genes in humans. He is a pioneer in using this information to help prevent diseases and other health problems.

JOHN KERRY
1943
BORN: Aurora, Colorado, USA

ROLE: Kerry was a Veteran protester who in 2013 became US Secretary of State in President Barack Obama's government. As Senator of Massachusetts, he worked with other veterans to help the US re-establish normal diplomatic and trade relations with Vietnam by the mid-1990s. He narrowly missed becoming President in the 2004 elections.

Did You Know?

Kerry is married to Teresa Heinz who is heir to the Heinz family fortune made from selling tinned foods such as baked beans!

BACK TO VIETNAM

Some Vietnam War protesters returned to Vietnam to help improve the lives of people affected by US military action. Chuck Searcy was a veteran who worked in business after the war but then returned for a tourist trip in 1992:

It was on that trip I realized that not only did the Vietnamese not hate us … they were very forgiving. But they were also still recovering from devastation of the war. We covered the whole country from north to south and it was at that point I decided to try and come back and make some kind of contribution that would be constructive rather than destructive.

Chuck worked with the Vietnam Veterans' Memorial Fund to start Project Renew. Its aims are to not only remove unexploded bombs and landmines from Vietnam, but also to help the Vietnamese injured by these weapons since the war, and to support small businesses. Find out more about Project Renew at www.landmines.org.vn/index.html.

▼ Mine detection in an area of Quang Tri, Vietnam, in 2006 funded by the US Vietnam Veterans' Memorial Fund. Between 1975 and 2004, in this area alone, over 10,000 people were victims of landmines and ordnance left over from the Vietnam War.

CHANGING PROTEST

Some Vietnam War protesters fought for other causes after the war. In 1968, a group of Catholic priests, including Daniel Berrigan, made napalm at home to burn draft cards in a Maryland protest. Daniel was arrested and spent three years in prison. In 1980, he and others broke into a factory making nuclear weapons to protest against their construction and use. They damaged nuclear warhead cones and poured blood onto documents. Daniel spent a decade in prison for such acts of civil disobedience.

Joan Coxsedge, who helped form SOS in Australia, dedicated herself to protests about women's rights issues after the war, such as contraception and abortion. She eventually became a politician. Bunyan Bryant attended University of Michigan teach-ins as a student but later became a professor there. His subject is environmental justice, which means, for example, defending people affected by environmental problems caused by others.

HISTORY DETECTIVES: CITATIONS

We all like to be credited for what we have achieved. Acknowledge individuals or groups whose primary and secondary sources you have used by listing them in a bibliography. Entries are generally arranged in order of author surname. This is followed by the title of the book or web page, the date of the book or article or web page access, and sometimes the number of pages. Here are some examples of how to cite different sources:

Book:
Becker, Elizabeth. *America's Vietnam War: A Narrative History*. New York: Clarion, 1992. p. 211.

Newspaper article:
Groom, Winston, "For Vietnam Today: A Hand Up", *Minneapolis Star Tribune*, 24 November 2000, 35A.

Website:
The Vietnam War, 1961–1970. Accessed 14 December 2000. Available from www.multied.com/vietnam.

WHY WERE THE PROTESTERS SIGNIFICANT?

Vietnam War protesters made it clear to their political and military leaders that the truth of events during war cannot be suppressed. They said that the death of protesters and war-time atrocities are unacceptable to a free American society. Their efforts and the media coverage contributed to the United States eventually ending its involvement in the war. One legacy of the protests has been increased questioning from the US public about their country's role in global politics.

WAR PROTESTS SINCE VIETNAM

In the 1980s, the Cold War continued with unprecedented military spending. Some historians and politicians put forward a revised version of what happened in Vietnam. In this, the United States lost the war because interference by anti-war protesters had prevented soldiers from

▼ Veterans protest on The Mall, Washington, DC in 2008 against further US involvement in the war in Iraq that had lasted five years at that point.

VIETNAM VS IRAQ

Many people have seen similarities between US involvement in the
Vietnam War and the war in Iraq. Both were long conflicts that
America did not win. There are many differences, however, such
as the respective causes of each conflict, and the use of the draft in
Vietnam. What similarities and differences can you find?

doing their job. This idea was popularized in films of the time such as
Rambo: First Blood Part II, featuring a lone Vietnam veteran taking it upon
himself to liberate prisoners of war from Vietnam. War protest became
unpopular.

Matt Southworth was 19 when he was sent to fight in the Iraq War in 2004.
While there, he saw sights that made him protest against the war. But at
school, he remembers that:

> [A]ny time someone brought up anti-war protests ... a lot of my
> teachers explained that away as a byproduct of [drug] usage in
> a crazy generation ... I didn't even realize there was an anti-war
> movement when I signed up.

Fewer people join anti-war movements today than during the Vietnam War.
One reason is that today soldiers have signed up for service rather than
being drafted in to fight. Another is that governments control access to the
military, as well as what journalists are allowed to report. In 1991, President
George Bush banned filming of returning body bags and injured troops
from the Iraq war to prevent public outrage.

TODAY'S PROTESTERS

However, there are still protesters questioning today's wars. In May 2012,
about 75,000 people took part in a protest march in Chicago against the
Iraq and Afghanistan wars. One of the many veterans who threw away their
medals in protest was combat medic Jason Hurd: "I'm here to return my
Global War on Terror Service Medal in solidarity with the people of Iraq and
the people of Afghanistan. I am deeply sorry for the destruction that we
have caused in those countries and around the globe."

▲ Kim Phuc Phan Thi in 2012, signing a copy of the photo that made her famous and inspired thousands to join anti-war protests.

EXPOSING THE IMPACTS OF WAR

Vietnam War protesters alerted the world to the impact of US weapons on Vietnam. For example, pressure from veterans' organizations encouraged Congress to give millions of dollars towards cleaning up Agent Orange. The number of landmines left after wars, which kill or maim around 26,000 people annually, appalled protester Bobby Muller. In 1992, he launched the International Campaign to Ban Landmines (ICBL). Over 120 countries have signed up to the campaign. Many mine victims are children, who often stumble upon landmines while playing.

Several charities provide help for children who are injured, orphaned, or made refugees as a result of war. One of these is the Kim Foundation run by Kim Phuc Phan Thi, who was the victim of a napalm attack when she was a child (see page 36). She managed to survive her injuries and rebuilt her life in Canada. She was made a UNESCO Goodwill Ambassador in 1994 for dedicating her life to promoting peace.

CONTINUING RESEARCH

In 2002, academic Nick Turse was digging through military documents in the US National Archives while researching for a dissertation. He found a folder from the early 1970s that detailed hundreds of incidents during the Vietnam War when US soldiers had attacked civilians and villages without provocation. Protesting veterans had mentioned such incidents during the war but there was little proof. Nick went to see his university professor:

> *[He said] get down there right away before these records disappear... I put every cent [I had] into copying ... from the moment the Archives opened in the morning until they kicked me out at night... [S]ometime after I published my first article on this, the records [disappeared] from the Archives' shelves. And they haven't been on the public shelves since.*

New primary sources still emerge not only about the Vietnam War but about today's wars, too. In July 2010 during the war in Afghanistan, the organization WikiLeaks published an online document called the *Afghan War Diary*, which contained over 91,000 secret military reports. Rather like the Pentagon Papers, the Wikileaks release had a big public impact and embarrassed the US military.

HISTORY DETECTIVES: FINISHING RESEARCH?

Every piece of research comes to an end. Perhaps the researcher has a deadline, perhaps he or she cannot find any more sources to look at. Yet new sources do emerge – sometimes years after historical events – that help to clarify what happened and why. Anyone starting to research a topic that has been studied and written about by many others should always remember – he or she might discover something new that adds to our understanding.

TIMELINE

1887	France makes Vietnam its colony
1940	Japan occupies Vietnam with French collaboration
1945	Ho Chi Minh's forces end Japanese occupation; declare Democratic Republic of Vietnam. French forces move in.
1950	Ho's regime receives military help from China. US pledges aid to the south.
1954	Ho's forces defeat the French; Vietnam is temporarily divided into North and South. French forces agree to leave.
1955	South Vietnamese leaders declare their country the Republic of Vietnam. Ngo Dinh Diem is president.
1961	US establishes the Green Berets in North Vietnam
1962	US first uses Agent Orange
1963	South Vietnamese forces loyal to Catholic President Diem attack Buddhists. A monk sets himself on fire in protest.
1964	*May:* First major demonstrations against the Vietnam War take place in New York City
	Aug: Gulf of Tonkin incident leads to President Johnson drafting Gulf of Tonkin Resolution
1965	*Mar:* US starts Operation Rolling Thunder; SDS organizes the first teach-in; the first US combat troops arrive in Vietnam; President Johnson authorizes use of napalm
	Apr: SDS and SNCC co-ordinate a march on the US capital
	Jul: President Johnson increases the draft
	Aug: Report by Morley Safer shows US Marines burning the village of Cam Ne

1967	**Jan:** McNamara launches ground operations
	Apr: 500,000 at marches in New York and San Francisco
	Jun: VVAW is formed

1968	**Jan:** Tet Offensive
	Mar: My Lai massacre
	Nov: President Nixon elected

| 1969 | Nixon approves secret bombing campaign in Cambodia |
| | **Nov:** US public learns of the My Lai massacre. 250,000-strong protest takes place in Washington, DC. |

| 1970 | **Apr:** US ground forces attack locations in Cambodia |
| | **May:** Kent State University protests end in four students being shot. Students are also killed at Jackson State University. |

1971	**Jan:** VVAW organizes investigations into US war crimes
	Feb: South Vietnamese and US forces invade Laos
	Apr: VVAW march in Washington, DC
	Jun: Pentagon Papers are published in the *New York Times*

| 1972 | **Mar:** PAVN crosses into South Vietnam |
| | **May:** Nixon launches aerial bombardment of the North |

| 1973 | **Jan:** Paris Peace Accords signed; US Congress abolishes draft |
| | **Mar:** Last US troops leave Vietnam |

| 1974 | North Vietnam resumes war |

| 1975 | **Apr:** South Vietnam surrenders to the North. Saigon becomes Ho Chi Minh City. |

| 1976 | Vietnam is unified as the Socialist Republic of Vietnam |

| 1977 | US President Carter pardons all Vietnam War draft evaders |

| 1997 | US and Vietnamese co-operation is resumed |

| 2006 | Declassified documents reveal further confirmed atrocities by US troops in Vietnam |

GLOSSARY

Agent Orange poisonous chemical used by US military in Vietnam to deprive the enemy of food and of hiding places in the jungles, by killing all vegetation. It got its name because of the identifying orange stripe on drums it was stored in.

allies countries that co-operate usually for military purposes, such as Germany and Japan during World War II

artefact human-made object. Artefacts are a type of primary source for historians.

atrocity wicked or cruel act such as a massacre

booby trap device such as a landmine that is intended to harm, surprise, or kill a person or people

chemical weapon weapon that works by releasing harmful chemicals

civil rights rights of citizens to political and social freedom and equality. In the 1960s, civil rights for African Americans were a major issue in the United States.

Cold War period of hostilities between the United States and its supporters and the USSR and its supporters based on differences in political systems as well as territorial disputes

colonization send people to a country to establish political control over it

communism political theory in which a state's property is publically and not privately owned. Wealth is divided among citizens equally or according to individual need. There is great control by the state.

court-martial military court set up to try military personnel for alleged offences, which can sometimes result in punishments such as imprisonment or even execution

draft when a government instructs particular citizens to fight in a war

evacuate when people are instructed to leave an area rapidly owing to imminent danger, such as an attack or natural hazard

hippy in the 1960s, someone who rejected established institutions and values, and lived an alternative lifestyle

landmine hidden explosive designed to injure enemy troops and damage vehicles passing over

moratorium suspension of an activity, such as a war

napalm sticky chemical often containing fuel. It was used by US troops in Vietnam to start fires and to injure the enemy.

pacifist someone who is opposed to violence as a way of solving disputes

patriotic when someone is devoted to and strongly supports their country and its actions

post-traumatic stress disorder (PTSD) mental illness that affects many combat veterans, which in previous eras was called "shell shock" or "combat fatigue"

probation period of supervised good behaviour

teach-in extended political protest at a university campus involving lectures, discussions, and other means of public involvement

tour of duty period of active service for a member of the US armed forces

USSR Union of Soviet Socialist Republics, the communist state that existed between 1922 and 1991. Modern-day Russia was part of the USSR.

veteran in military terms, someone who has fought in a war

Vietcong name given to the National Liberation Front (NLF) and North Vietnamese fighters. *Vietcong* means "Vietnamese Communist", although most NLF members were not communist and were simply against the South Vietnamese regime.

FIND OUT MORE

BOOKS
Non-fiction
The Vietnam War (Living Through), Cath Senker (Raintree, 2012)
Vietnam War (Facts at your Fingertips), Leo Daugherty (Wayland, 2011)

Fiction
Goodbye, Vietnam, Gloria Whelan (Random House, 1993)
Old Man, David Poulsen (Dundurn, 2013)
Vietnam, Book 1: I Pledge Allegiance, Chris Lynch (Scholastic Press, 2011)

WEBSITES
www.archives.gov/education/research/primary-sources.html
Do you want to know more about finding primary sources? Visit the
US National Archives website.

www.bbc.co.uk/schools/gcsebitesize/history/mwh/vietnam
The BBC GCSE Bitesize web pages include short videos explaining the
reasons why the United States went to war, the different methods of
fighting, and what happened after the war.

www.loc.gov/vets/stories
The Library of Congress website "Experiencing War: Stories from the
Veterans History Project" has a page on Vietnam War participants, with
links to fascinating interviews, diaries, and other primary sources.

**news.bbc.co.uk/1/shared/spl/hi/asia_pac/05/vietnam_war/html/
introduction.stm**
The BBC's history of the Vietnam War contains lots of useful information.

DVD
Good Morning Vietnam (directed by Barry Levinson, 1987, rated 15)
This is a funny film about a radio programme for US troops in Vietnam
that addresses the horrors and also the boredom of being a soldier in
that conflict.

OTHER TOPICS TO RESEARCH

There are many different interesting topics related to the Vietnam War. Why not try investigating one or more of the ideas given below?

- Mothers' groups:
  Another Mother for Peace is a mothers' group mentioned in this book. But there were other such groups active in the United States during the Vietnam War, including POW/MIA Families for Immediate Release and American Gold Star Mothers. How were the aims and membership of these groups different?

- Technology and protest:
  Research the role of technology such as social media in spreading protest during recent conflicts and other events. For example, you could look at how Iranian youth used social media during the elections in 2009, in a protest movement which is sometimes called the Twitter Revolution.

- Anti-war protest:
  Anti-war protest movements have existed long before Vietnam, going back at least to World War I. Research the history of anti-war protests in the United States and in the United Kingdom.

- Ho Chi Minh Trail:
  Today, many tourists visit this trail, a former supply and troop movement route for North Vietnamese forces during the war. Find out more about the route and its importance for the eventual North Vietnamese victory and for decisions made during the war by US military leaders.

INDEX